Weird Bugs

Einstein Sisters

KidsWorld

The Atlas moth is the **largest** moth
in the world. Its wingspan is more than
25 centimetres. That's **bigger**
than a **dinner plate.**

Atlas Moth

In **Taiwan**, the **cocoons** of Atlas moths are used as purses.

The Atlas moth doesn't have a mouth. It only **lives** for a **week or two** after coming out of its **cocoon**.

This moth lives in Southeast Asia. It is **common** in **Malaysia**.

The **ferocious** water bug is
a large water beetle.
It is also called **"toe-biter."**
Its bite is painful but **not**
poisonous.

Ferocious
Water Bug

When these bugs go underwater, they store air under their wings so they can breathe while they are submerged.

The female lays her eggs on the male's back. He takes care of the eggs until they hatch.

When it is attacked, the ferocious water bug plays dead until the predator goes away.

There are **more** than **500 kinds** of bombardier beetles. They are **found** all over the world.

Bombardier Beetle

When this beetle is threatened, it shoots a **boiling hot** chemical **spray** from its **bum**. It can **shoot** more than **20 times** in a row and fire in different **directions.**

The **hot spray** comes out with a hissing or popping sound. It can **kill** small insects and even **burn human skin.**

The cockchafer is a kind of beetle. It is also called "May bug" or "doodlebug."

Males have seven "leaves" on their **antennae**. Females have only six.

Cockchafers make a loud whirring noise when they **fly**.

Cockchafer

These beetles spend three or four years underground as **larvae**. They **eat** the roots of plants and can **damage** farm crops.

Army Ant

There are more
than **200** kinds of
army ants. Some **live**
in **Africa**. Others
live in **Central** and
South America.

As the ants **march** along, they **eat** any insects, spiders, snakes or **lizards** that get in their way. The ants **climb trees** and shrubs and sometimes even **go through houses.**

Army ants **don't** have a **permanent home** because they are **always moving.**

Army ants live in **groups** called colonies. A colony can have up to **700,000 ants.**

Dung beetles make pieces of poo into **balls**. They **roll the balls** around with their **back legs**.

Each type of dung beetle only uses the **poo** of **one** kind of **animal**.

Dung beetles steer their balls by using the stars.

The male dung beetle rolls the ball. The female either rides on the ball or follows behind.

Dung Beetle

Cicada

Cicadas spend **most** of their time underground as **larvae**. The fully grown beetles **emerge** after **13 or 17 years.**

Male cicadas gather in large groups in trees. They make loud buzzing and clicking noises to attract females.

Cicadas drink tree fluids, so they pee a lot. Cicada pee is called "honey dew" or "cicada rain." Wear a hat if you walk under a tree full of cicadas!

Cicadas have two large eyes that are usually red. They also have three more tiny eyes called "ocelli" between the two main eyes.

Asian Giant Hornet

The Asian giant hornet is the **largest** hornet **in the world.** It lives in **eastern Asia.**

Giant hornets are **dangerous.** Their stinger injects a **strong poison** that many people are **allergic** to. About **30 to 40 people die every year** from hornet stings.

This hornet **eats other insects.** It also **steals honey** from beehives.

The **giant hornet** is about the **size** of an adult's thumb.

The giant **weta** is also called
"wetapunga."
It is most active at **night**
and **cannot fly.**

Giant Weta

There are more than **70 kinds of weta.** They all **live** in **New Zealand.**

To grow, a weta must **shed** its hard outer "**skin.**" It sheds its skin **11 times before** it is fully grown.

A **giant weta** can **weigh** as much as **three mice.**

Orchid Mantis

The orchid mantis is white or pink. It **hides** among **orchid** flowers. The lobes on its **legs** look like flower petals.

The orchid mantis is a **kind** of praying mantis.

The **female** orchid **mantis** is about as long as an **adult's** little finger. The **male** is only **half as big.**

This mantis stays **very still** until an insect comes by. Then it **strikes** quickly to **catch** and **eat** the insect.

This spider looks like a pile of bird poop. Its camouflage keeps birds and other predators from trying to eat it.

Bird dropping spiders build horizontal, triangular webs with sticky threads that hang down. Insects walking by stick to the dangling threads, then the spider pulls them up and eats them.

Bird Dropping Spider

Bird dropping
spiders **live** in
Southeast Asia
and **Japan**.

This spider **glows**
under **ultraviolet**
light.

Camel Spider

These spiders eat insects, **lizards,** small birds and **mice.**

Camel spiders are also called "**sun spiders**" or "**wind scorpions.**" They live in **dry, desert areas.**

The **largest** camel spiders are about as long as a five-dollar bill. They can **run faster** than an **adult human.**

Even though camel spiders **look scary,** they **aren't poisonous.**

The Goliath beetle is the **largest** beetle in the world. Some **beetles** are **longer,** but they are either lighter or not as strong.

Goliath Beetle

There are six kinds of Goliath beetles. They all live in Africa.

A Goliath beetle can lift a load that is 850 times heavier than its own weight. That's like a human lifting a jet plane.

The beetle's hard outer shell protects its delicate wings.

Firefly

Fireflies **are winged beetles.** Some people call them **"lightning bugs."**

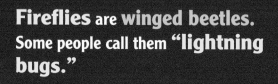

Even firefly **eggs** and **larvae glow.** Firefly **larvae** are called **glow worms.**

Fireflies **talk** to each other by **flashing their lights.**

Chemicals in the **firefly's body** produce the **light.** It is a **cold** light and doesn't give off any **heat.**

Giant African Millipede

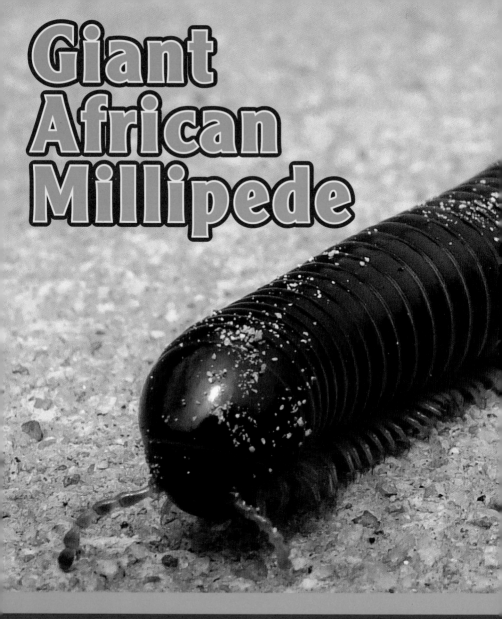

The giant millipede is **longer than a ruler** and about as **thick as an adult's thumb.**

The name **millipede** means "thousand legs," but these creatures usually **only have 256 legs.**

Millipedes have **two sets of legs on** each **body section.** The legs all move **independently.**

Millipedes eat dead leaves and other **decaying plant matter.**

The treehopper's colours and shape help it hide from predators.

There are **3200** kinds of treehoppers. They usually look like thorns, buds or other parts of plants.

Treehoppers **drink sap** from plant stems.

Treehopper

Female treehoppers are **good mothers**. After the **young hatch**, she **watches** them to make sure none **wander off** and get **lost**.

Bullet ants **live** in the **jungles** of **Central and South America.**

The **bullet ant** has a very **painful sting.** Some people say that it is like being **hit by a bullet,** which is how the **ant got its name.**

Bullet Ant

Bullet ants
eat insects.
They also **drink**
nectar and sap.

The bullet ant is one of
the **biggest** ants
in the **world**. It is about
2.5 centimetres long.

Velvet Worm

The velvet worm's **body** is covered with tiny, **bristly scales**. They make the **worm's** skin **velvety** and **waterproof**.

Velvet **worms** have between **13** and **43** pairs of feet.

The velvet worm can **shoot sticky slime** from two "**cannons**" on its head. The slime **traps insects** so the worm can **eat them.**

Most velvet worms **don't lay eggs.** They **give birth** to live young that look like miniature **adult worms.**

Assassin
Bug

There are **more**
than **6000** kinds
of assassin bugs.

The assassin bug hides until an insect walks by, then it jumps out and **injects** the insect **with poison.** The poison **turns the insect's insides to liquid** so the assassin bug can **suck them out.**

Most kinds of assassin bugs **eat** other insects. Some eat the **blood** of **birds,** reptiles or **mammals,** including humans.

The puss caterpillar got its **name** because it is **cute and furry**. It is usually **golden brown**. It can also be **pale or dark grey**.

Puss Caterpillar

The **caterpillar's** "**fur**" is actually made of **sharp spines**. The spines carry a strong **poison** that causes **severe pain** to anyone who **touches them**.

This caterpillar becomes a **flannel moth**.

Rhinoceros Beetle

Rhinoceros **beetles** are some of the **largest** beetles in the world. There are more than **300** different kinds. They can **grow** to be 15 centimetres long.

Rhinoceros beetles **can't fly very well because** they are **so big.**

Male rhinoceros beetles use their horns to fight other males. They do not bite or sting humans.

This beetle makes a hissing or squeaking sound by rubbing its wing covers on its abdomen.

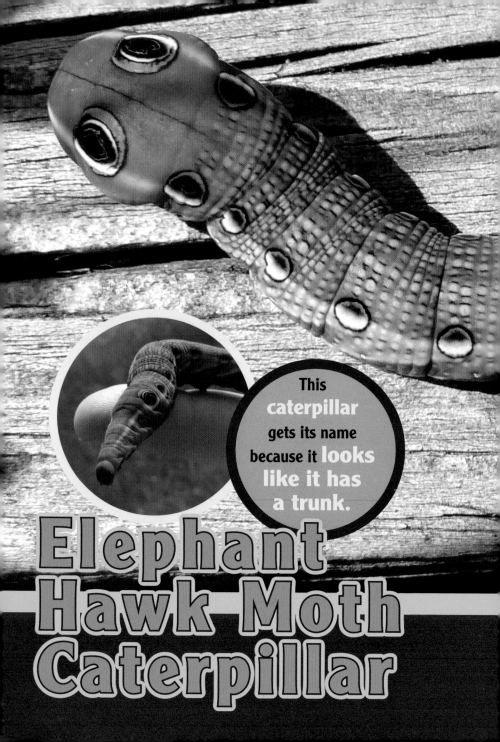

This **caterpillar** gets its name because it **looks like it has a trunk.**

Elephant Hawk Moth Caterpillar

The caterpillar's snake-like appearance scares away birds that might eat it.

This caterpillar can make itself look like a snake with a large head. It has four patches that look like eyes.

It turns into an olive green and pink moth.

The giraffe weevil lives in Madagascar. It was only discovered in 2008, so scientists don't know very much about it.

The female only lays one egg. She rolls it up in a leaf to protect it.

Giraffe Weevil

Male giraffe weevils use their long necks to fight with each other.

The male weevil's body is about as long as an almond, but its neck is about two times longer. The female has a much shorter neck.

Glasswing Butterfly

This butterfly lives in Florida, Mexico and Central America.

Butterfly **wings** are usually covered with **tiny, colourful scales.** The glasswing butterfly's wings only have scales **around the edges,** so the rest of its **wings** are transparent.

The **transparent wings** help the butterfly **hide** from **predators.**

The **Spanish name** for this **butterfly** is *espejitos,* which means "little mirrors."

The end of the scorpionfly's tail
looks like the stinger of a scorpion,
but it is **harmless.**

Scorpionfly

The scorpionfly uses its **long beak** to eat dead insects. It often **steals its food** from **spider webs.**

Scorpionflies **have been around** for about **250 million years.** They are the **ancestors** of modern moths and **butterflies.**

Hummingbird Moth

This moth **flies** and **moves** just like a **hummingbird**. It can **hover** in front of a flower while it **drinks nectar**. It even makes a **humming sound.**

The moth's long, thin **drinking tube** is called a **"proboscis."** The tube **curls up** when the moth **isn't drinking.**

Unlike most moths, the hummingbird moth is **active during the day.**

The hummingbird moth helps pollinate flowers. Pollen **sticks** to the moth's **fuzzy body** and is carried to other **flowers.**

This spider is
a kind of **tarantula**.
It is the **largest** and
heaviest spider
in the world.
It is as **big** as
a dinner plate.

This **spider** is found in **South America**. It lives in a **burrow** in the ground.

Goliath bird-eating spiders don't actually eat birds very often. They eat **earthworms, insects, frogs, small snakes, lizards** and **mice.**

Females can live for **25 years.** The males only live for **three to six years.**

Goliath Bird-eating Spider

Velvet Ant

The velvet ant isn't really an ant—it's a kind of **wasp**.

Velvet ants sometimes make a **squeaking sound** if they are disturbed.

The velvet ant has a **very painful sting**. Some people call it "cow killer," but **no cows** have ever been **killed** by this **wasp**.

Most velvet ants are **bright red** and black, but they can also be **black, white, silver** or **gold.**

A monkey hopper is a kind of **grasshopper**. It lives in **tropical parts of the world.**

It is also called "matchstick grasshopper" because of its **skinny back legs** that stick out **sideways.**

Monkey Hopper

**Monkey hoppers
eat mostly ferns.**

Pillbug

Pillbugs aren't really bugs. They are **crustaceans,** like **lobsters** and **shrimp.**

A pillbug can **drink** **with its bum** as well as its **mouth.**

Pillbugs **have** **blue blood.**

The **pillbug** is also called "woodlouse," "sowbug" or "roly poly." It curls into a **tight ball** when it **feels** **threatened.**

A **tardigrade** is only about the size of a **poppy seed**. The **best** way to look at it is **through a microscope**.

Tardigrades are nearly indestructible. They can live in **boiling water**, in **solid ice**, deep in the ocean and in **outer space** where there is **no air**. They can also survive **high levels of radiation**.

Tardigrade

There are more than **1000 different** kinds of tardigrades.

Tardigrades are also called **"water bears"** or **"moss piglets."**

The Publisher: KidsWorld Books

Library and Archives Canada Cataloguing in Publication

Weird Bugs / Einstein Sisters.

ISBN 978-0-9940069-4-3 (pbk.)

1. Insects—Juvenile literature. I. Einstein Sisters, author

QL467.2.W4 2015   j595.7   C2015-901210-4

Cover Images: Front cover: rhinoceros beetle, victor zastol'skiy/Thinkstock. *Back cover:* bombardier beetle, seanjoh/Thinkstock; giant weta, Sid Mosdell/Flickr; tardigrade, Darron Birgenheier/Wikipedia.

Background Graphics: abstract background, Maryna Borysevych/Thinkstock, 3, 19, 29, 31, 41, 45, 53, 55, 63; abstract swirl, hakkiarslan/Thinkstock, 38; pixels, Misko Kordic/Thinkstock, 5, 6, 7, 8, 11, 15, 16, 17, 20, 27, 28, 32, 35, 37, 40, 41, 42, 46, 47, 51, 52, 54, 56, 58, 59, 62.

Photo Credits: From Flickr: Benny Mazur, 44–45; Br3nda, 18; David Hill, 6; gailhampshire, 8; Geoff Gallice, 36, 43, 59b; Graham Wise, 33; Kathleen Franklin, 57; Matthew Robinson, 5; Miguel Perez, 32a; NH53, 48–49; Rain0975, 40–41a; Roy Niswanger, 39b; Sid Mosdell, 18–19; Steve Jurvetson, 31b. *From Thinkstock:* AndreAnita, 13; Atelopus, 34–35; dalhethe, 53; dr322, 47; FourOaks, 12–13; Frederico Arnao, 40; genphoto_art, 32b; Hemera Technologies, 26, 27; ivkuzman, 29; kivandam, 50; kororokerokero, 28; Mathisa_s, 2–3a; Miyuki Satake, 60–61; Morley Read, 10, 37; Musat, 15, 38–39; NokHoOkNoi, 3b; pum_eva, 9; seanjoh, 6–7; suwich, 22–23; Thomas Quack, 52; victor zastol'skiy, 42; webguzs, 35b; Wirepec, 14. *From Wikipedia:* Axel Strauss, 46; Bjorn Christian Torrissen, 30–31; Braboowi, 25b; Carrascal, 58–59; Craig Pemberton, 56; Daniel Mietchen, 62b; Darron Birgenheier, 62–63; David Tiller, 49b; Greg Hume, 4; Jean Pierre Hamon, 45b; JonRichfield, 24–25a; KENPAI, 16–17; Luc Viatour, 21; Mehmet Karatay, 11; Mikkel Houmoller, 51; Patrick Coin, 41b; Phillip Psurek, 20; Snakecollector, 54–55.

We acknowledge the financial support of the Government of Canada through the Canada Book Fund (CBF) for our publishing activities.

Canadian   Patrimoine
Heritage   canadien

PC: 30